FAMOUS AIRCRAFT:

The B-24 LIBERATOR

by Steve Birdsall

A Len Morgan Book

ARCO PUBLISHING COMPANY, INC.
219 Park Avenue South, New York, N.Y. 10003

ACKNOWLEDGMENT

The compilation of this book has been an involved task, and if it is successful it is very largely due to the efforts of the people who have assisted me. I would like to thank the pilots, all those who supplied the photographs appearing here, Allan G. Blue and d'E. C. Darby, two foremost Liberator experts, Kenneth T. Crothers, historian for the 11th Bomb Group Association and a wonderful source of 7th Air Force history, Jerzy B. Cynk, O. T. Flieg, Philip Moyes, John Preston, J. Rabbets and the South African War Museum. And thanks are also due four people who have catered to my every whim over the past year — Roger Freeman, Royal D. Frey, Colonel C. V. Glines and Lt. Colonel Robert A. Webb.
S.B.

CONTENTS

. . . in the eye of the beholder

With a name no less inspiring than Flying Fortress, and probably a shade more precise, the Liberator came and went in considerably less time. When the B-24 appeared, the need for multi-engined bombers had already been proved. There were no headlining mass flights, no glamorous advocates fighting an uphill battle for strategic airpower. In essence, the B-17 had fought the major prewar battles for both types of heavy bomber. In the deadlier encounters that followed honors were far more closely divided.

The obvious preference of several commanders, including such notables as General James Doolittle, for the Fortress did not help the Liberator's reputation, and was too often contagious. Fledgling aircrew who had flown neither type had an inbuilt preference for the B-17.

But if this reads as a prelude to the justification of the B-24, it is not meant to. This rather premature comparison of the two bombers is the only concession made to the enduring practice of doing just that. There are no apologies made, none necessary. The pugnacious Liberator was a great aircraft, individual in both appearance and performance. Its adaptability was almost endless — the aircraft was a superb long range transport, an excellent reconnaissance aircraft. No mean feat for a bomber design. It served both the Americans and the British exceedingly well, along with Australia, Canada, South Africa and probably Germany, although they had only a few . . .

Some of the pilots' opinions that are gathered here align, others do not. In many cases this stems partly from the different models of the B-24 they flew, and the variety of operating conditions and tactics employed.

"and Roosevelt became angered and spake unto

the Killer across the waters. And Killer became angered and went among his second lieutenants and others, smiting them with his rod line. And upon every man he smote there grew a pair of wings ... and Killer smiteth Ordnance, commanding them, 'putteth one thousand pound bombs into their pockets.' And they did so ... the Killer flieth his men over Napoli time after time ... his men crieth 'pray our master returneth us home for we are tired.' But they crieth in vain ... and Roosevelt spake unto Congress and Congress spake unto War Department and War Department spake unto Cairo H.Q. and Cairo H.Q. spake unto Killer saying, 'Cut off ye wings of they who have required number hours.' And he did so, weeping and gnashing his teeth. But the men were happy for they were as ground grippers."*

Killer Kane.

"A mental journey back across a quarter of a century to the days of World War II is not easily accomplished. So many pictures flash across the mind, dim and out of focus. One is constant — the ungainly looking airplane with the twin tail, the B-24 heavy bomber.

"Long since relegated to the scrap heap, abused, discredited, maligned, and bastard step brother to the B-17, this good and faithful servant is long overdue a few kind words.

"Other men are more capable of painting pictures with words or describing the feelings of others, but few or none have lived for hours on end flying over oceans, deserts and mountains, through fog and ice and tropical storms, through combat ... as one who flew the B-24, I'm happy to have this chance to express my feelings about our grand old airplane.

"From the earliest days fighting men have had little choice in their weapons. In 1941 I was Operations Officer of a B-17 squadron, although not a pilot. Major was the minimum rank for four-engine pilot rating. This changed rapidly, but I, along with many others, was spilt off to form new units with B-24s. We liked the Liberator better than the B-17 ... it performed better, was more maneuverable, and as we gained experience as pilots we felt capable of accomplishing our tasks with the new airplanes.

*From "Low Level Mission," by Leon Wolff.

"The B-17 was an old rocking chair plane flown with the ailerons. The B-24, with high lift wing and twin stabilizers, was sensitive about the loading around the center of gravity, but properly flown could carry the largest load higher, faster and much greater distances than the B-17. It could also be operated under field conditions that stopped the B-17, and when not forced to operate with slower B-17 formations could out-perform the Fortress in every way. The 8th Air Force in England, equipped with both, forced the B-24s to fly behind the B-17s at an airspeed and in a flying position entirely contrary to the designed performance of the B-24. Consequently the Liberators suffered from loss of maneuverability, stability, and were too close to stalling speed to afford a very high safety factor when damaged by enemy action. The losses of B-17s could be offset by pointing to those of B-24s; however, the resulting publicity may have helped the morale of the B-17 men but it did nothing for those who flew the maligned and misused B-24.

"Credit has never been given for the outstanding performance of the B-24 in every theater of war, nor for its varied capacities from hauling fuel to keep tanks rolling to resupply by parachute to submarine patrol, transport of VIPs, long range radar sniffers, naval recon, weather flights, and the freezing of ice cream for local messes. Until the B-29 the B-24 was the most modern aircraft with the latest equipment. Without detracting from the B-17 it should be made part of the enduring record that the B-24 did its fair share and was an outstanding success at the work for which it was created.

"In times agone I heard ad nauseum that the B-17

Hovering under their fighter cover, two Second Air Division B-24s head for Cologne. The aircraft on the right is fitted with a BTO installation in place of the ball turret. (USAF)

The 446th Bomb Group in formation. Bernard Hutain is flying HN-M, the Werewolf. (USAF)

"Grumpy", of the Disney-dominated 343rd Squadron, 98th Bomb Group, was Colonel John R. Kane's Ploesti aircraft. (USAF)

"Snow White" of the 343rd was lost to enemy aircraft during the August 1, 1943 mission. (USAF)

was the better bombing platform. I had experience with bombing from both and can only say that good bombing can be done from either. In my group, the 98th, we consistently flew over targets in Italy above 25,000 feet; quite often the top squadron would be above 30,000. These missions were to drop bombs on ships or docks located 800 to 1000 miles from our base and took from twelve to sixteen hours flying time in formation. One reason we had less than desired results on some bombing missions — failures to drop into the pickle barrel — was the faulty design of our bombs. Army Ordnance designed bombs and all data was obtained from drops from 10,000 feet, and bombing tables made from such data. No supersonic wind tunnels existed in the U. S., and we found that our bombs behaved erratically when dropped from over 25,000 feet. Our calculations showed that the bombs reached the speed of

sound before contact but we never did learn just what happened to throw them off target.

"A large part of press comment was devoted to the invulnerability of the B-17. With due credit to the Fortress, the B-24 sustained as much battle damage and returned from combat in such a condition that only the skill of the crew brought it back to base. After all, it was quicker to fly than to swim! This contrast of two airplanes reminds me of two mothers on the verge of fisticuffs over whose son suffered the worst wounds in combat."

Colonel John R. Kane's name is not unfamiliar. He led his 98th Bomb Group, "The Pyramiders," in the 177 aircraft attack on the Ploesti oil installations on August 1, 1943. He is recorded as a commander who knew exactly what he wanted from his men and planes, and usually got it. After twenty years he has become quite lyrical about the old B-24. The 98th

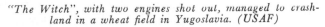

"The Witch", with two engines shot out, managed to crash-land in a wheat field in Yugoslavia. (USAF)

"Prince Charming" went down in flames shortly after "The Witch." (USAF)

"Teggie Ann", returning from the Ploesti mission on August 1, 1943, served with the 376th Bomb Group. On the mission she carried General Uzal G. Ent and Colonel K. K. Compton and made the wrong turn which is credited in most circles as the main cause of the Ploesti slaughter. A B-24D, 42-40664, the aircraft was painted desert pink overall, with yellow edged national insignia and white aircraft numbers. (USAF)

and 376th Bomb Groups had been pulled out of the Sicilian campaign in July, 1943, to train for a low level strike at Ploesti, Rumania. To bolster the force two 8th Air Force groups, the 93rd and 44th and the new 389th Bomb Group were transferred temporarily to the Ninth Air Force. An intense ten-day training period began. Formation minimum altitude flying, attack after attack on a replica of the target laid out in the desert, and two full dress mock missions. In the early morning on August 1 they headed north over the Mediterranean then northeast across Albania, Yugoslavia and Bulgaria. Sixty-five miles from the target they slipped down to 500 feet. A miscalculation took the leading 376th group off course to the outskirts of Bucharest, alerting the defenses. When the 98th reached their targets, followed by the 44th, they found the 93rd had been there first. They ploughed through the fire and the explosions of delayed action bombs. Kane's plane, "Hail Columbia," the aircraft he had fllown as commander of the 344th squadron and which had been renamed "Grumpy" with the 343rd before being renamed "Hail Columbia" for the Ploesti·mission, was hit in one engine as it came over the target. The heat was unbearable, and the turbulence inside the fire and smoke was a pilot's nightmare. All but eight of Kane's force got over the target, one having cracked up on takeoff and seven others turning back with mechanical troubles. They had the worst losses of all — 21 of 38 that arrived at the target were knocked down. Kane himself wound up crash landing spectacularly in Cyprus. Fifty-four aircraft were lost. Often called a disaster, the mission has gone into history with other bloody aerial engagements like Schweinfurt — Kane himself compared it to the Charge of the Light Brigade. He was one of five participants in the mission who received the Medal of Honor — one 44th, two 93rd, and one 389th. Only three more Medals were won in Liberators, and yet another of these went to the 98th's Lt. Donald Puckett, over Ploesti in July 1944. One went to the 308th's Maj. Horace Carswell, who singlehandedly attacked a Japanese convoy in the South China Sea in October 1944, and Lt. Col. Leon Vance, of the 8th's 489th Bomb Group in June 1944.

The choking skies of Ploesti were a world away from Smyrna, Tennessee, where Bob Carlin had his first ride in a B-24:

"Everything was so metallic, and reverberated with solid sounds. The brakes hissed like a huge truck, and we bobbed stubbornly as we taxied. I couldn't believe the damned thing was going to aviate.

"We were really busy — too darn busy — and had a gang of meters to read, always at the wrong times. It was customary for the flight engineer to stand between the seats and call out the air speed; otherwise it would mean eyes off the runway, on the air speed, back to the runway, etc., and getting that bird off was an eyes-out-front deal.

"Once airborne the airplane assumed a certain grace and didn't behave badly at all, but this changed again when formation flying started. It was brute force handling for all minor adjustments. As a matter of fact one day I was outside our tent in the spring sun shaving and my co-pilot suddenly noticed I was all lopsided. Sure enough, I had developed a

This photograph was taken just after Lt. Carlin landed #951 on a partisan airstrip at Zara, Yugoslavia on March 1, 1945. Approaching the field the crew saw the burning B-24 landing and had to follow — all fuel was gone and number one was feathered. Carlin left the power on so the turrets could swivel, and they were trained on the truck that approached. It turned out to be Yugoslavian. Gilbert Lewis, a photographer, was with Carlin's crew, and he ran back to capture the scene. The Spitfires in the background are Balkan Air Force, fueling and arming; they had just landed. The following day #951 was patched, fueled and flown out. On the way back number one went again. The 456th scrapped her. (Robert Carlin Collection)

This is the full ground crew of a South African Air Force Liberator VIII based in Italy. (S.A. Official Photo)

sizable muscle under my arm on the left side only. This was my flying arm, while my right arm was used for throttles — no effort.

"On my first mission, to Brux in Czechoslovakia, I flew old 293, the 'Worry Bird,' the worst airplane ever built. Came back with one dead engine, and another at 25% and vibrating. It finally went down six weeks later with another crew."

Lt. Robert Carlin flew thirty-two missions with the 747th Squadron of the 456th Bomb Group. Between that first mission on December 23, 1944,

"Lazy Lou" of the 446th Bomb Group.   Her yellow and black tail markings had recently replaced the H in a white circle marking. She went down soon after this photo was taken. (USAF)

and his last on April 26 of the following year, he has some recollections:

"In all we lost sixteen engines, but not all to battle damage. One out was OK. Trim or autopilot could hold against the turning impulse, but two out on one side was a horror. We went through this once. We had dropped our bombs and were just making it on the other two, but were pushing it. But both trim and auto wouldn't hold it straight. I put both feet on one pedal, and when my legs began to burn I used my hands to push down on my knees to keep them from buckling. For three and a half hours we struggled, going down hill all the time. It was all tension and teeth gritting agony. We made a three and a half hour approach to our field and I had to be helped out of the seat. For a week after that I kicked down oak trees for fun . . .

"The nose wheel doors on our B-24s were pushed open by the emerging wheel, and very minor springs snapped them shut as the wheel retracted. We lost a bombardier who put his chest pack chute up for a pillow en route home and settled back for a comfy ride while reading some magazines he had taken along. The chute was right on the doors, and we saw him go as the doors opened beneath his weight. He was spread eagled, pants flapping, and magazines fluttering behind him. The unwary were claimed quickly.

"The Liberator would not land wheels up. It would squash. Also, if ditching, the top turret would tear loose and hurl down between the pilots' seats.

"Towards the end of the war we got B-24s with ball bearing controls. I went down and picked up a replacement at Bari and on takeoff I damned near turned a loop. I was expecting the usual wrestling match and the controls were feather light.

"We finally learned how to land the 24. Just before flare out we would crank the nose up with trim and then hold against it if necessary. Sure beat the massive manual effort.

"But I think I can truly say that I'm glad I had a chance to drive one of the old agony wagons, they sure made pots and pans out of them in a hurry after the war.

"Naturally in our own right we were pretty hot pilots. Our formation flying got so good that the lead ship tail gunner would depress his guns, the slot man's nose gunner would elevate his, and they'd screw them together. And no one ever changed a wingtip light on the ground! We would put our wing tip in the open waist window of the ship next door and the gunner would perform the task."

Carlin has more stories of intricate maneuvers, but they have been excluded as they have not yet been officially verified as true. On the subject of vivid memories of B-24 days, he has this to say:

"Two fighters came up at 6 o'clock low, punched a few holes and shot past on our left. Both were standing on their right wingtips and the leader was a Spitfire! His wingman was an Me 109. The Spit was lustre black, with crosses. Wonder who he was? One day we headed back to base after takeoff to allow all others to form on us — we were leading the mission — a B-24 from another group had taken off, cleaned up all gear and flaps and started to bank toward his squadron. He just kept going until it became a vertical turn; and then so gracefully arced down to a thunderous crash right below us. He had a belly full of frags and when we got home at 4

Ie Shima, 1945. The war was almost over, and the B-24's task. (USAF)

James Stewart with members of the 389th Bomb Group in Norfolk. (Gerry Collins Collection)

Many people think of James Stewart more as the pilot of the *Spirit of St. Louis* or the flying wreck of *Flight of the Phoenix* than an Eighth Air Force Liberator. Brigadier General James Stewart joined the Army in 1941 as a private, and was commissioned in 1942. He completed basic and advanced flight training and then instructed in AT-9s at Mather Field, California. He was a pilot in Bombardier Training School at Kirtland for six months before being transferred to Hobbs for four-engine training. An instructor on B-17s, he went to Gowen Field, stayed there for nine months, and was then made squadron commander of the 703rd Squadron of the 445th Bomb Group at Sioux City . . .

"I put the B-24 to a severe test one night in Iowa: I was making a landing in a thunderstorm and, between lots of lightning and some bad judgment on my part, I flew the poor bird into the ground at 120 miles an hour. The nose wheel gave way and was never found again, but, other than that, she just bounced and settled down with a groan.

"I remember the B-24 very well and, although it came out of the war with a rather questionable reputation for some reason I think most of those who flew the airplane have a very soft spot in their hearts for the machine.

"I learned four engine operation in the B-17, but while I was instructing in that airplane the change was suddenly made to the B-24; the transition didn't seem at all difficult, which speaks well for the bird.

"In combat, the airplane was no match for the B-17 as a formation bomber above 25,000 feet, but, from 12,000 to 18,000 feet the airplane did a fine job."

In the fall of 1943 the 445th moved to Tibenham, in East Anglia, as part of the 8th Air Force. In all, General Stewart is credited with twenty combat missions, all as command pilot. He led the 2nd Combat Wing — the 389th, 445th and 453rd groups — to Berlin on March 22, 1944. Early in 1944 he transferred to the 453rd Bomb Group, one of the 445th's two sisters, as group operations officer. He returned to the States as a full Colonel in 1945.

p.m. they were still smoking in hundreds of little fires. Just thought of how we lost an engine on take-off, pruned an olive orchard, threw the bombs right through the bay doors — the added drag of an open bomb bay at 30 feet altitude would have finished us. We were too busy to be scared. Back in the tent we spent a solid day in silence."

"Red Ass" from the 446th heading for Hanau on November 10, 1944. This plane led the D-Day bombers, Barney Hutain recalls. (USAF)

A 461st Bomb Group B-24M during the group's last operation: to supply the Spittal POW camp near Villach, Austria, on 9 May 1945. (Stan Staples)

Lumbering characteristically, B-24s of the 461st Bomb Group taxi out at Torretto. Aircraft 36, a B-24L, is fitted with the manual tail turret which was 200 lbs. lighter than the previous one. In the background are aircraft of the 484th Group, with bow-like fin symbols, sharing the base. (Stan Staples)

Little knowing that Lt. Robert Carlin was winning the war a few miles away at Stornara, Lt. Stan Staples was working toward the same goal with the 461st Bomb Group at Torretto, Italy. From his reminiscences it is possible to gain an insight into the fundamentals — some of them — of flying the B-24.

"The flight deck was quite large and comfortable. The seats were easy to sit in for hours, and the deck was large enough so that you could stand up and move around a bit after several hours at the controls.

"The 24 was a bit awkward to board, especially in combat gear. Here we dressed in heavy high altitude flying clothes, with the bulky wired pants and jacket over the regular uniform plus Mae West and chute harness. We looked like a bunch of overgrown Teddy Bears, and it was somewhat of a chore to squat down, bend over, slide under the open bomb bay doors, stand upright, lift a leg onto the catwalk, then crawl up onto the flight deck. It was almost as much effort, after an 8-10 hour mission, to reverse the procedure and haul oneself back out. Certainly none of the jaunty gymnastics of the B-17 crews."

Staples recalls the Liberator as being "a pleasure to fly, generally quite responsive on the controls, although a little sluggish when fully loaded, and particularly at altitudes over 24,000 feet, the handling began to suffer."

"Coming to the outfit near the end of the war, November 1944, we didn't see much fighter opposition. Once in a while they'd hit us, but generally it was just one fast pass through the formation with the P-51s right behind them. We feared flak most,

and there was generally no shortage . . . I have my Purple Heart to prove it. Structurally the plane was sound, a fact I learned the hard way. We were on instruments after takeoff, climbing up through to form on top. Evidently a ship passed in front of us and we hit its turbulence. Our ship went over on its back, spilled the flight gyros and went into what must have been the graveyard spiral, because the airspeed began to build. We recovered control just as we broke the cloud base, going almost straight down.

"Going back over my photos certainly brings back memories. Caught myself daydreaming a couple of times and I would swear I could hear the starting up of the engines, number 2 first, because it had the generator to supply the rest of the power, then 1, then 3 and 4. I can still feel the vibrations as the cylinders fire, then catch, followed by the big belch of light gray smoke swirling from behind the cowlings. I remember how we used to sync the props by leaning our heads back so that we could watch the shadow pattern of the blades. If the shadow moved toward or away from you the engines were not on the same rpm, but when the shadow stood still, the rpm were synchronized and the engines would purr."

Although condemned to an early death in this flying purgatory, the B-24 men decided to make the best of it. The mechanics who stood on the slippery Davis wing in English winter, Pacific monsoon or North African oven, the aircrew who rode the ship to places they can't remember how to spell, and as already written here, liked the aircraft. They embellished them with names, and some of the most beautiful art of all appeared on B-24s in the Pacific. In the far-flung garrisons were some renditions still could not appear here, even after over twenty-five years of relaxing morals. Some carried these names into history, and their names gave them their individuality. "Witchcraft" of the 467th Bomb Group flew 130 missions and dropped half a million pounds of bombs, "Club 400" of the 15th's 454th Group flew 115, "Gone With the Wind" of the 90th flew over 100, and "Form 1-A" of the same group flew 161. "Embarrassed" of the 380th flew 108 and sank three ships and "Blue Streak" of the 376th made 110. "Lady Corrine" of the 456th had flown 155 before being taken into Russia. In 100 missions "Lil Audrey" of the old 11th Bomb Group's 431st Squadron flew 225,000 combat miles, took one crew through forty missions, and another through thirty. Once she put twenty hours of flying in one 24 hour period — commendable on her 94th and 95th missions! Once she came home with her nose flaming, another time, when her main hydraulic line was severed, the crew used grapefruit juice and drinking water in the leaking system, pumped the flaps and wheels down manually and rigged three parachutes in case the brakes didn't hold. They did.

Barney's Buzz Wagon was the second aircraft assigned to Captain Bernard L. Hutain of the 8th Air Force's 446th Bomb Group.

The first, the *Werewolf*, had gone down with another crew, and the name of the second was a tribute from his crew, who had seen the tree leaves stuck in the bomb bay doors or stood aside as spray showered through the waist windows as the props churned the water a few feet below, while their pilot had a high time with the aircraft.

"No matter how you looked at it those twin elongated rudders just made it an ugly plane," he recalls. "The high wing, the large oval fuselage, the disproportionately large twin rudders with no grace or style seemed to overwhelm you with its mass or bulk, way out of proportion to its true size and weight. No one ever *wanted* to fly the B-24. It was the worst thing that could happen to you as a newly graduated pilot. After AT-9s, it was a difficult airplane to transition to, heavy on the controls, sluggish to respond, and difficult to get the feel of. Even after you checked out you drove the B-24 rather than flew it for the first fifty hours anyway. Some pilots could never master the 24 as aircraft commanders and were relegated to co-pilot positions. As

Known as "First Sergeant", this war weary B-24D became the assembly ship for the 458th Bomb Group. (USAF)

a matter of fact, my own co-pilot was trying to transition to a/c and on his first or second flight as a/c lost an engine and in what should have. been a "normal emergency" turned into his dead engine and crashed in the middle of Denver, killing all on board. He just never mastered the high wing loading, high stallability of the B-24. It was very easy to get into a high speed, or secondary, stall. The Davis Wing was no doubt a good design but it was a high speed wing and you had to be careful not to pull too many gs in a turn or pull out, or you would find yourself in a secondary stall quite easily. The B-24 was essentially too underpowered for the Davis Wing. No doubt as it was originally designed the power and wing were a good combination, but add nose turrets, armor, belly turrets and so on and the engines just couldn't pull the ship through the air fast enough for efficient aerodynamic handling. When the bomb bay doors were opened at high altitudes the airplane could almost be said to have stopped flying and merely mushed through the air. Our bombing altitudes were almost always 4-6000 feet lower than the B-17s'. The B-24s did fly faster — they had to to merely stay in the air. The narrow chord wing also meant that C.G. travel was much more critical.

The 24 was a much harder airplane to fly in formation — as you slowed down a little the nose would have to be raised proportionately higher to maintain a given height, then when it was necessary to speed up the initial power application would only serve to lower the nose, then more power to increase the speed to catch up to the leader. By this time the aircraft would want to accelerate too much tending to overshoot the leader — so off with the power again just as you really got to a more efficient altitude — but now the plane wants to keep going — so off with more power — but now you've taken off too much. Worse still, your leader has now slowed down himself or made another turn — and so on for eight hours more or less."

If it was difficult to maintain formation, it was even more difficult to initiate it. Barney Hutain likens it to Russian roulette, with the English bases overcast to varying degrees on nearly every mission. Organizing the bombers, with each plane and pilot an individual with different performance, when they had clawed their way to clearer skies was another part of the chore. The 446th used, after intricate flare signals proved less than perfect, an old war weary they had dubbed "Fearless Freddie." The air-

craft was painted with large black and white checks and orange fins with a black horizontal stripe, and was one of many used throughout the Second Air Division.

Hutain continues: "I disliked the B-24 for a long time, but as I gradually learned to fly it I found myself becoming fond of the ship, if not exactly loving it. You learned to anticipate its sluggishness;

The 445th Bomb Group's formating aircraft carried red stripes and a multitude of lights, but no armament. (USAF)

A B-24J-25-CO and a B-24J-35-CO of the 308th Bomb Group heading for targets in the Hunan province of China. (USAF)

you learned to fly it right up to a hairline from a secondary stall — in formation you learned to make many minute power changes at the slightest hint of acceleration or deceleration, instead of wide open throttles alternated with closed throttles because there didn't seem any in between way of doing it. To sum up, it was a difficult airplane to fly, but like many other things, if you ever mastered it, you could take special pride in yourself — a good B-24 pilot was a good pilot. All I've said is from a beginning pilot's standpoint, but the average B-24 pilot with our group went on the plane with about 240 hours — his so-called multi-engine training in a worthless Cessna AT-17 — and he'd be on his way overseas with maybe 100-200 hours on the plane, and I'd say it took 400-500 hours to learn to like the 24, and fly it easily and efficiently. I flew my first mission on December 22, 1943, and my last on June 28, 1944 — thirty in all."

Climax is defined as culmination, or apex — the peak. Authors like to build up to it, and the story of Lieutenant Robert Strong and his Liberator provides a fitting climax to this little sentimental journey.

"Most of us have referred to our B-24 as a flying boxcar and often commented that it glided like a rock. Although not endearing terms for a fine airplane, each pilot would hasten to challenge derogatory comments from an outsider, and call their attention to at least one fateful mission when this faithful bird refused to die."

Bob Strong has a fateful mission of his very own.

The 11th Bomb Group had been fighting the Japanese since Pearl Harbor, first in B-17s, then B-24s. The tide had turned by the time Strong reached the group's 42nd Squadron in the Marianas. The 42nd had been assigned the special task of laying then secret 1000 pound aerial mines in the Volcano and Bonin Islands prior to the Iwo Jima invasion. The tide had turned, but there were still some hairy experiences to be had. On the second of thirty-four missions, on November 29, 1944 ... but better to let Bob Strong tell the story:

"That was my first low level mine laying mission to Chichi Jima. Previous attempts to close the channel between the south edge of the mine field and shore had failed due to the cliffs at the shore's edge. Based on information from previous missions, it was decided that a flight of four planes would come in over the high cliffs at the south end of the island, fly in tight formation down a narrow canyon which pointed directly at the mine field, and all crews would drop their loads at a signal from the lead crew. It amounted to turning a Liberator into a Mitchell.

"As the lead ship flew lower and lower, the formation came closer and closer to avoid the walls of the canyon. The ground fire was so intense over the target that the midair collision was not apparent to Lieutenant Robinson's crew or mine, until we returned home. We both assumed that flak had rolled up my wingtip and caved in the side of his bombardier's compartment. In the next instant, with my plane rolled on its left side and Robinson's directly above, his bombardier staggered to his feet and toggled the mine release button on signal from the leader. The first of his three mines entered our plane through the side of the fuselage between the waist window and the tail section. The drop chute, which was attached to the rear of the mine and was actuated as the mine left the airplane, was billowed out to full size and acting as an efficient brake behind the plane. Between that chute and our jammed control cables the plane continued on a rapidly descending course toward the water, not many feet below.

"Quick action of the crew in cutting the chute shrouds and brute force on the controls finally stopped the descent. Then at full power, in an unusually nose high attitude — the mine lying in the very rear of the fuselage caused us to fly like a paper bag full of water — we started a very slow climbing turn out of the harbor. Within fifteen minutes of the target the crew managed to pry the mine up and out through the same hole it had entered, using the barrels of the waist guns as levers. We noted the drop point for our own shipping, and we started to sweat out the 800 miles to home. The auto-pilot, which had been impossible to use on the trip north because of erratic operation, was engaged to reduce fatigue and operated as smoothly as a symphony orchestra. The tail section was in a state of continuous motion which caused a crack to start up the side of the fuselage. We watched the tail section shear off as mile after mile the crack continued around the fuselage. Then as a result of many prayers and a well built airplane the crack was turned at the longeron and started toward the rear of the airplane. We sat the plane down on Isely Field like we were flying a cracked egg, and taxied to the hardstand we'd left the day before. The plane was so badly damaged and out of alignment that it ended up in the boneyard, but a successful mission had been accomplished, and from that day on through my 34th and final mission, which ended up with crash-landing a badly shot-up plane on Saipan, I was convinced that Liberators were the best damned airplane in the world."

Captain Jesse E. Stay, commander of the 42nd Squadron, had looked at 377, shaken the loose, rattling tail assembly. "Damned if I know how he ever got it back," he said.

Back from Chichi Jima and a memorable mission, Lt. Strong's 377 bares her damage to an incredulous 11th Bomb Group. (11th Bomb Group Association)

The XB-24. (Convair)

BUILDING A BOMBER

Mr. Davis said: "The full benefit of my aerofoil can be obtained only if the entire ship be designed around it."

The unmistakable Davis Wing first appeared on the Consolidated Model 31, basis for the XP4Y-1 flying boat, and was the salient feature of Model 32, the Liberator bomber. The wing's high lift was claimed as reducing drag by twenty-five percent at low speeds and ten percent at high speeds. This was combined with Fowler Flaps, which slid back and down on tracks, increasing wing area in the extended position, for better low speed performance.

In early 1939 the Air Corps was seeking an aircraft with better range and more performance than the B-17. They wanted 3,000 miles range, over 300 mph and a ceiling of 35,000 feet. With 39-680, the shining XB-24, they would get the range, but a top speed of only 273 mph.

Isaac M. Laddon, Consolidated's chief engineer, had nine months to put the design into flying form. He did just that. Laddon had joined Consolidated in 1927, and had been chief design engineer during production of the XPY-1 flying boat and the PBYs. He was appointed executive vice president and general manager in 1941, and is now a director of General Dynamics Corporation.

Initial specifications were completed in January 1939, and a mock-up of the Liberator was prepared. Wind tunnel tests were carried out the following month, and in March the contract for the prototype was signed.

The XB-24 was 110 feet long, with a wingspan of 63 feet. The aircraft was powered by four Pratt & Whitney R-1830 engines, each turning out 1200 hp from their fourteen cylinders. The bomb bay had a capacity of 8,000 lbs, and was divided into front and rear compartments, with the bombs stowed vertically. The roller-shutter type of bomb bay doors retracted upwards, and produced little additional drag. Armament was light — only six .30 caliber hand-held Brownings.

The aircraft first left the ground on December 29, 1939, at Lindbergh Field, San Diego. The man at the controls was William B. Wheatley, and his workout with the ship fulfilled most expectations. A batch of seven YB-24s were already ordered, along with thirty-six B-24As, but while the tests were successful, the Air Corps wanted refinements. The seven

Isaac M. Laddon. (Convair)

YB-24s differed from the prototype in having de-icer boots on the wings and tail, and gross weight increased by 5400 lbs to 46,400 lbs.

The Consolidated XP4Y-1. (Convair)

AM262, one of the six LB-30As, became G-AGHG after this photo was taken. (BOAC)

The first production Liberators, called LB-30As, went to the British. AM258 was the first of six, almost exact duplicates of the YB-24. These first British Liberators were used as transports on the Return Ferry Service between Prestwick, Scotland, and Montreal — nearly 3,000 miles. The first was

AL579, one of the 139 Liberator IIs, served with the RAF in the Middle East, first with 159 Squadron, and later 160 Squadron. (Imperial War Museum)

August 10, and twenty-two more died in a similar accident four days later. But the remaining four aircraft, carrying the civil registrations of BOAC, carried on.

Next were twenty Liberator Is, which went to RAF Coastal Command after being embellished with aerials and four 20mm cannon. They went to 120 Squadron first, in June 1941, and their range proved them invaluable.

At that time the USAAF was accepting its first B-24A, one of nine. Thirty-eight had been ordered but the balance were converted to later models on the production line. These aircraft carried six fifty caliber machine guns, with two .30s in the tail. In July Lt. Colonel Caleb V. Haynes took an Air Corps Ferrying Command B-24A across the North Atlantic and in August he and Major Curtis E. LeMay pioneered the South Atlantic route. In September two other B-24As, clearly marked with large flags of a then neutral United States, took part of the Harriman Mission to Moscow by way of England. One went on from Russia through the Middle East, India, Singapore, Australia, New Guinea, Wake and Hawaii. The other came back through Egypt, Central Africa, the South Atlantic and South America.

The Liberator II was a model unique to the RAF, its extended nose section adding thirty-one inches to the plane's length. Two Boulton-Paul four gun .303 caliber turrets replaced some of the hand held guns, one turret in the mid-upper position, the other in the tail. The British received 139 Liberator IIs, but fifteen were taken over by the USAAF and went to the 7th Bomb Group in the Pacific when Japan struck at Pearl Harbor — at that time the USAAF had only nine B-24As.

159 and 160 Squadrons of Royal Air Force Bomber

announced to have flown the Atlantic on March 24, 1941. Twenty-two people were killed when one of the aircraft crashed into a hillside on takeoff on

AL504, Churchill's "Commando", was modified almost to RY-3 standard at San Diego in 1944. (RNZAF)

A fine example of the B-24D was "Chug-A-Lug" of the 98th Bomb Group, with 105 missions. Like her sister ship, "The Squaw", she came home for a Bond Tour. (USAF)

Command became the first bomber units to use the Liberator, and Liberator IIs also equipped three squadrons of Coastal Command. Some of them, unarmed, went to the Return Ferry Service and BOAC and later Qantas. The aircraft, serialled AL 503 to AL 641, produced one of the most famous Liberators of all, AL 504, Winston Churchill's "Commando."

Two B-24As had been scheduled to fly reconnaissance in the Pacific area over Japanese installations in the Marshalls and Carolines, particularly Truk, but only one had arrived in Hawaii when the Japanese attacked, and this machine, 40-2370, was destroyed at Hickam Field.

The XB-24 had been reworked into the XB-24B, with self-sealing tanks, armor, and turbo-superchargers. This increased the speed to 310 mph. Nine B-24Cs resulted, with the Martin dorsal turret and Consolidated tail turret, each with the twin fifties which became a standard armament in USAAF bombers.

Then came the B-24D. 2,425 were built in San Diego by Consolidated, 303 by them at Fort Worth, and ten by Douglas at Tulsa. The first B-24Ds had only a hand-held nose gun and four more guns in two turrets. Later aircraft were fitted with a single ventral gun, firing through the camera hatch, and still later two more nose guns were added, plus two waist

"Connell's Special", a veteran 90th Bomb Group B-24D, was converted for gunnery training of B-29 crews early in 1945. (Ray Pritchard)

San Diego's production line in full swing. The machines are B-24J-120-COs, a block which accounted for fifty of the 4,350 B-24Js built by Consolidated. (Convair)

guns. Ten machine guns in all. Bomb load was increased to 12,800 lbs, and absolute maximum gross weight climbed to 71,200 lbs and the hand held gun was replaced by a Sperry ball turret with twin .50s. The RAF received B-24Ds as Liberator IIIs in mid-1942, with Anglicized armament. Some were Lend Lease Liberator IIIAs with American equipment, and nearly all went to Coastal Command, some becoming G.R.Vs. Their radar gear included retracting chin and ventral radomes and the sub-spotting Leigh Light fitted under the right wing, and some had provision for eight rockets. The USAAF used a number of B-24Ds for similar work, and the Navy received some as PB4Y-1s. But the B-24D was only the beginning of the Liberator as a bomber.

In other roles the B-24Ds became the first C-87 Liberator Expresses. The British called them Liberator C.VIIs and their capacity was twenty passengers and a crew of five. Five became AT-22 trainers, and later TB-24s. The Navy called theirs C-87s RY-2s. A VIP version, with ten berths and a galley, became the C-87A and Navy RY-1, and one C-87A, 41-24159, called *Guess Where II*, was built expressly for President Roosevelt. He never did use it, but Mrs. Roosevelt did in March of 1944.

The C-87 had been the result of a crash landing of a Liberator early in 1942. The aircraft was repaired and flown to San Diego, with fixed landing gear. There Laddon and an Air Force representative supervised a three week modification. "We did it mostly by waving our arms and pointing to show where we wanted equipment taken out, a deck laid, or openings cut," Laddon recalls.

The B-24E was little different from the D, and one of these was modified in late 1943 as the fuel-carrying XC-109. Its purpose was the immense logistical problem involved in the B-29 campaigns from China. Range and capacity made the B-24 a natural choice. Metal nose and bomb bay tanks were fitted, with a 2900 gallon capacity. 2900 gallons that could be pumped out in just one hour! The B-24Ds and Es that became C-109s were modified to carry flexible bag tanks. Another B-24D became the XF-7, with extra fuel tanks in the bomb bay and eleven cameras.

Yet another B-24D became the XB-41, a bomber escort equipped with fourteen guns and 11,000 rounds of ammunition. Additional upper turret, chin turret and twin waist guns were the main features. The aircraft was never tested operationally, and probably just as well.

The vulnerability of the B-24D to head-on attack — not the exclusive problem of the Liberator of course — had resulted in various placings of twin guns in the nose. In a central ball joint, a lower ball joint, or side by side; but these were still precious little for the nose gunner to hide behind. Some 11th Bomb Group B-24s were equipped with twin waist

A C-87 at Shanghai's Kiangwan Field in 1946, prior to transfer to the Chinese Air Force. (Dave Lucabaugh)

"Frenisi" of the 307th Bomb Group, a B-24D fitted with the Consolidated tail turret — at both ends. This aircraft flew its hundred missions and was awaiting the beginning of a Bond Tour when this picture was taken. (USAF)

guns in the Pacific, but the recoil was tremendous and the fitting never became standard. A more successful armament modification was the latter day fitting of a 20mm cannon in the nose of VPB-108 Privateers. This had a singularly destructive and demoralizing effect on enemy anti-aircraft batteries.

The third producer of the Liberator, Ford at Willow Run, began with B-24Ds — 480, as B-24Es. In all 791 B-24Es were built, and the British called this model the Liberator IV, although they were only paper airplanes, the RAF receiving none. The XB-24F was a B-24D with thermal de-icing in place of

the standard boots, but the model never reached production. The Thermal Ice Preventative System was introduced on later B-24Js, using a system of hot air ducted along the leading edges, and this was the XB-24F's legacy.

North American began building Ds without the ball turret as B-24Gs, and these were the first aircraft to be fitted with a nose turret in place of the hand-held guns. The first Liberator with a nose turret was modified in Australia by 5th Air Force engineers—it bore the tail turret from another D grafted neatly into the nose. Similar work was done by the 7th Air Force and both became supplied with modified aircraft from the Hawaiian Air Depot.

The nose turret increased the aircraft's length by 10", and the production turrets used were Emerson,

A B-24M-35-CO with the Chinese Air Force at Haneda Airport, Tokyo, in October 1946. (Dave Lucabaugh)

Consolidated, and Motor Products designs. There were 6,678 B-24Js in all, the most numerous mark of all. The B-24J was so similar to its immediate predecessors, the B-24G and B-24H, that some of these were redesignated B-24Js. The British and Commonwealth Air Forces called the B-24Js Liberator Bs or G.R.VIIIs, and about 1200 went to the RAF. Some B-24Hs became F-7s, and B-24Js F-7As and F-7Bs, both with six cameras in various positions. The Navy called all their B-24s PB4Y-1s, but their B-24Js had the Aerco nose turret, which was distinctive by its circular shape.

The B-24L was similar to the J, with a lighter tail turret to improve handling, and a few were modified to train future Superfortress gunners and were called RB-24Ls. They were equipped with remote controlled guns — with radar they became TB-24Ls.

Last of the main line was the B-24M, with a power tail turret. Later came the XB-24P, a modified D, which was allocated to the Sperry Gyroscope Company for fire control research. The XB-24Q was a B-24L with radar controlled tail installation of the kind used in the B-47. Not overshadowed by these was the result of Wright Field discussions that brought forth the grafting of a B-17G nose on a B-24J, in June 1944. The bird was found to be "operationally unsuitable"—who knows what weird mutations might have followed had this not been the case.

It had been reasoned long before that the B-24 would be more stable with a single fin. In 1943 Ford had modified a B-24D as the XB-24K, and it certainly did have improved stability and control. In April 1944 it was decided that future Liberators would be minus the twin tail, and the XB-24N and seven YB-24Ns resulted before Liberator production ceased on May 31, 1945. The B-24N orders were cancelled but the Navy received 740 single finned Liberators as the PB4Y-2 Privateer, which had been contracted in May 1943. This aircraft was heavily modified — seven feet longer, with two upper turrets and twin-gun waist blisters. The transport version was called RY-3, and the RAF received twenty-seven as the Liberator C.IX. The distinctive oval cowlings, necessitated on the B-24 by the supercharger installation — the oil coolers were placed each side of the engine — were installed vertically instead of horizontally in the PB4Y-2, and 1350 hp engines were used.

AL547, built as a Liberator II, was one of four operated by Qantas. As G-AGKU, she was broken up in Sydney in December 1947. (Qantas)

Consolidated's very heavy bomber was the B-32 Dominator, and a generalization could be to call it a Super Liberator, capable of carrying a ten ton bomb load against a target 1250 miles away. The reversible pitch propellers and Davis Wing fitted the aircraft to SWPA landing fields, and tests were begun in 1944. Only General Kenney seemed interested, and test crews were pessimistic about the first three aircraft, but General Whitehead thought them very suitable for the job at Okinawa. On recommendation, the 312th Bomb Group became the first B-32 unit, but only one squadron had converted by VJ day and only fifteen of their aircraft actually saw service. On August 17, 1945, four 3rd Bomb Group B-32s, flying one of the first missions from Okinawa, were attacked by fighters while reconnoitering Tokyo. On the 18th they were attacked again, and in the last two days of the war shot down three enemy aircraft.

The Model 39 was originally designed as a fat bellied single tailed variant to serve as a Navy cargo

The XB-24N, the Air Force's single-finned Liberator. (Convair)

plane, the R2Y-1. The Navy ordered 250 in 1943 and the prototype flew on April 15, 1944, but the order was cancelled. It was decided to adapt the plane as Convair's first post-war commercial transport.

Stripped of the second upper turret, Privateers of VP-23 formate over Miami in July 1949. (USN)

There were 2,567 B-24s at Kingman, Arizona in 1946. This 389th Bomb Group veteran is one of them. (William T. Larkins)

In the summer of 1945 Convair and American Airlines outfitted the plane as the Liberator Liner for co-operative research in shipping cargo by air. On 37 flights 283 tons of cargo was handled, from magazines to strawberries, and meteorologists charted temperature forecasts for various altitudes along the route — the shipper and flight captain then picked altitudes to suit — 55-60 degrees for ripening cargo, 40-46 to keep it unchanged.

After the war the USAAF had little use for the B-24, and 5,518 went to the Reconstruction Finance Corporation. By 1951 only one appeared on the USAF's inventory, a B-24M. The RAF used Liberators in various post-war roles, including troop carrying and aerial surveying until mid-1946. The Navy kept Privateers long after the war, some serving with the Coast Guard, and VW-3 and VP-24 were the last patrol and weather reconnaissance squadrons to operate them, in 1954. They painted them in a variety of colors — a PB4Y-2K was all red, an older PB4Y-1 used in missile experiments was all yellow. The Honduran Air Force got a few Privateers as demilitarized transports around 1958, and in 1957 four Privateers were bought by a Brazilian private company to be converted for cargo hauling. Only two were converted and flown, and one BuNo. 60001, still flies as PT-BEG. Most of the RAF's remaining B-24s went into storage after the war and were scrapped in the early fifties. Some were used as forest fire spotters, others as VIP and transport aircraft, and a few as fire-fighting training hulks. The Indian Air Force used bomber Liberators until the 1960s, but needless to say, there is a shortage of B-24s. Some of the inert aircraft that remain are collected in the following pages. Some Liberators still fly in the United States, most, if not all, ex-Navy PB4Ys, and a few PB4Y-2s still serve as firebombers in Oregon and Arizona.

"The Lady Is Fresh", a B-32 Dominator of the 312th Bomb Group, and one of the few to see combat at the end of the war. (USAF)

30

44-51228, a B-24M-21-FO, went on display at Lackland AFB in 1954 after duty with the Aero Icing Research Laboratory as an EZB-24. (Lackland AFB)

Tulsa International Airport, 1966. This aircraft has just forty-five hours flight time. It is a B-24J-20-FO, purchased by the Spartan Aircraft Company for training purposes and resold a few years ago. (American Airlines)

Languishing at the Air Museum in California, this B-24 wreck only saddens. (Steve Birdsall)

PB4Y-2 60001 in Brazil in 1957. The aircraft still flies, as PT-BEG. (Jose Ribeiro de Mendonca)

India was the last country to use the B-24 in the role it was designed for. (Indian Air Force)

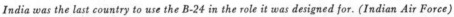

"Bolivar Jr" was donated to the 7th Air Force by Consolidated workers, and reached the 11th Bomb Group's 431st Squadron in the Marianas. (USAF)

THE LIBERATOR
GOES TO WAR

A rare photo of a 7th Bomb Group LB-30 in India. The 7th had a collection of B-17s and Liberators that ranged far and wide during the black, early days of the war. (Roger A. Freeman Collection)

Lush Java, rich in rice, timber, cinnamon, tobacco, tea, sugar, coffee and rubber, was one of the most valuable of the Dutch colonies in the Malay Archipelago. In January 1942 the Japanese were only a few weeks short of adding Java to their list of prizes.

On the sixteenth, at noon, three LB-30s and two B-17E Fortresses took off from Malang, Java, and headed for Kendari on Celebes. The LB-30s, AL 609, AL535 and AL576, were all Liberator IIs which had arrived from Africa just one week before.

At Kendari they took on their bomb loads and at 2:45 p.m. on January 17 the five bombers were droning toward the enemy airdrome at Langoan,

south of Menado, on Celebes, and shipping in Menado Bay. The three LB-30s were after the airfield.

Over the target the tiny formation watched their bombs fall on the runways and revetments, then lit out for Singosari field at Malang, glad of the extra miles per hour granted by their empty bomb bays.

AL609, commanded by Major Austin A. Straubel, made it, but AL535 and AL576 left him along the way. Lt. John Dougherty in 535 crash-landed on an islet off South Borneo, and eight days later a Catalina picked the crew up. The two B-17s, both damaged, made it as far as Kendari. One was wrecked there in a Japanese air raid, and the following day

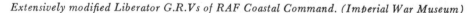

Extensively modified Liberator G.R.Vs of RAF Coastal Command. (Imperial War Museum)

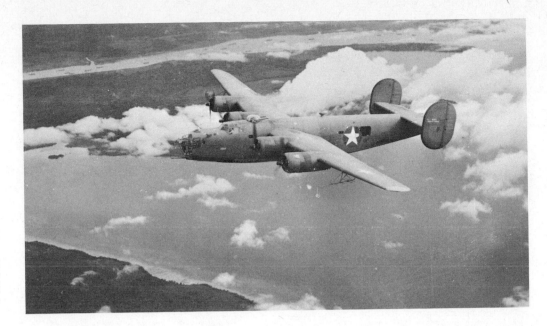

This VMD-154 PB4Y-1, 31940, was damaged early in 1943. After landing at Henderson Field, Guadalcanal, for quick repairs it returned to Espiritu Santo and during major repair it was fitted with a 37mm cannon, fired by the pilot. (Al Bibee)

AL 609 came up from Java and collected the crew.

Major Stanley K. Robinson's 7th Bomb Group had carried out the first American B-24 mission of the war. Losses: two LB-30s. Sixty-six percent.

Liberator Is had been operating with RAF Coastal Command's 120 Squadron at Nutt's Corner, Belfast, since June 1941, when their unequalled range had lent new potency to the command. Liberators were the only Very Long Range aircraft to comfort northern Atlantic convoys in mid-ocean, RAF and Royal Canadian Air Force planes flying from Iceland in

1943. Coastal Command put the Liberator II through its paces, and so did 159 and 160 Squadrons, the first Bomber Command units to operate the type, first against the Germans in the Middle East and later the Japanese in Burma and Malaya.

On October 9, 1942, Liberators of the 93rd Bomb Group filled out the 8th Air Force's first one hundred-plus bombing raid. Their first target was Lille. Over the next seven months they played their part in the attacks on the U-boat pens and yards at Lorient, Brest, St. Nazaire and Wilhelmshaven, but it

"Bolivar" flew 81 missions with the 30th Bomb Group, came home for a Bond Tour, but crashed at Downey, California. (USAF)

Back from the Bay of Biscay, a Navy Liberator spends some rare time over land in February 1944. (USN)

was not until May 17 that the Liberators operated independent of the Fortresses . . . and liked it. Thirty-four gray-bellied aircraft from the 44th and 93rd Groups attacked Bordeaux, roaring out of the Bay of Biscay as they completed a sweeping 700 mile, three and one-half hour semi-circle. They took the German garrison completely by surprise. Flak was meager, and enemy fighter interception was one intrepid German who quickly joined the Eighth's collection of "probables." Their bombing was accurate, their navigation had been superb, and the mission was destructive. The lock gates were burst open, and the controlled water level tumbled out into the Garonne. A 1500′ pier was smashed, and direct hits dotted the aircraft engine factory. Back at the Liberator bases in Norfolk there was ill-concealed delight.

There was another way of getting at the U-boats, and Liberators were deeply involved there too. B-24s of the Army Air Forces Antisubmarine Command, in England since November 1942, were cooperating with Coastal Command, but the Navy felt these duties were in their domain, and finally they assumed the responsibility of antisubmarine work. By the end of 1943 three Navy squadrons were operating, and had behind them experience like that gained on November 10, 1943, in a truly allied operation. It began when an RAF Wellington raised the U-966 sixty miles off the Spanish coast at 4:00 a.m. By 8:00 a Liberator of VB-105 had arrived and made two strafing attacks, but the potent return fire crippled the PB4Y-1's release gear and ruined the bombing attack. An hour later a British fighter strafed the sub, and the Liberator riddled the conning tower before departing for fuel at 10:00. A VB-103 aircraft from Dunkeswell was called in and circled and strafed until 11:45 and dropped five depth charges that straddled the U-boat. She began to settle by the stern but kept going under an umbrella of thick flak. The PB4Y-1 headed for home at noon, but another, from VB-110, was aready on the way, and reached the scene thirty minutes later. After dropping six bombs he too left, at 1:15. An RAF Liberator with a Czech crew, probably from 311 Squadron, began a bomb run but was beaten off by the antiaircraft fire. They went in again and harried the U-boat all the way to the cliffs, where the crew abandoned ship under a rocket attack just before the submarine ran aground near Ortiguiera.

By mid-1944 there were eight USN PB4Y-1 squadrons flying from England under RAF control, and the 8th Air Force Liberators were occupied with the Combined Bomber Offensive. Although almost always overshadowed by the Fortresses in the 8th, they struggled, then strode, along the same path.

Other Liberators, flown by Poles and South Africans, were fighting another kind of war in August and September of 1944. The Polish 301 Squadron,

The 93rd's "Bomerang" was the first 8th Air Force Liberator to complete fifty missions. (USAF)

RAF, flew 97 sorties to Warsaw dropping arms to Poles who had risen against the Germans on August

B-24Hs of the 718th Squadron of the 449th Bomb Group, based at Grottaglie in Italy. (USAF)

A 389th Bomb Group B-24D undergoes engine repairs in England. The 389th, the "Sky Scorpions", flew with the 9th Air Force against Ploesti. (USAF)

1. Sold out by the Russians, they became one of the war's most tragic sacrifices. The Red Army, already at the doorstep of Warsaw, refused to let Allied aircraft land in their territory. Like vultures, they watched the slaughter, Stalin unbending to all pleas. The supply missions were suicidal— 301 Squadron, flying as "C" flight of 138 Special Duties Squadron, lost seventeen Liberators and Halifaxes. 148 Squadron, RAF, also suffered heavy losses before being withdrawn from the missions. The two South African Air Force Liberator Squadrons, 31 and 34, based in Italy, carried on, but 31 Squadron lost seven B-24s over Warsaw on August 13, 14 and 16, and in six weeks the squadrons had lost twenty-four of their thirty-three aircraft. The slaughter in Warsaw, and overhead, was one of the great tragedies of the war.

The Halverson Detachment was twenty-three B-24Ds that had been assembled to make a raid on Tokyo from China in the Doolittle tradition. Reaching Egypt, they were slated for one mission — an attack on Ploesti, Rumania. Twelve Liberators made the target at dawn on June 12, 1942, but damage was slight. The B-24s were then thrown against Rommel's advance. Their original purpose forgotten, these aircraft, and a few B-17s General Brereton brought from India, were the foundation of the Ninth Air Force. In July the 98th Bomb Group arrived in the Holy Land, and by spring they and the 376th, "The Liberandos," flying out of airfields in the Benghazi area, were making their presence felt over Naples and Messina.

The Liberators were pulled out of the Sicilian campaign in July 1943 to make ready for the low-level Ploesti mission. To build up the force the 44th and

A 356 Squadron Liberator B.VI near Mandalay. This squadron shared the greatest shipping prize in South East Asia, a 10,000 ton tanker, with 159 Squadron in June 1945. (Imperial War Museum)

93rd Groups were borrowed from the Eighth in England and the 389th Bomb Group was diverted from them to the Ninth. The five carried out July attacks on Rome and Naples before undergoing intensive training for August 1.

In mid-August, still recuperating from the bloody loss of almost one third of the Ploesti force, the five groups made the first attack from the Mediterranean on a target in greater Germany, bombing Wiener Neustadt with a force of 65 aircraft. Here they did achieve the elusive element of surprise, and only two aircraft were lost.

In September the three borrowed groups went to England, and in November the 15th Air Force came into being. By the middle of January 1944 six new groups, the 449th, 450th, 451st, 454th, 455th and 456th, equipped with B-24Hs, had arrived to join the 98th and 376th. The 449th Group sent twenty-seven of their freshly painted B-24s to knock out the enemy reconnaissance airfield at Perugia on January 19. Their sixty-five tons of bombs put the base completely out of action for the next four days and were largely responsible for the tactical surprise gained by the Allied forces at Anzio on January 22.

During the second half of 1944 the 15th began its offensive against oil targets like Ploesti, the refineries near Budapest and Vienna and the synthetic plants at Odertal, Oswiecim, Brux and Blechhammer. Ploesti was finally out by August 19, 1944 at a cost of over 350 bombers. The campaign never let up and Germany began the last year of the war with only four refineries and six ersatz plants to fill her empty planes and tanks and trucks. On March 15, 1945 the Fifteenth Air Force's final hammer blow against enemy oil fell when 522 Liberators and 225 Fortresses buried the Florisdorf refinery near Vienna under more than sixteen hundred tons of bombs.

The forbidding China-Burma-India theater saw its first mission by Brereton's 10th Air Force when three aircraft, one LB-30 and two B-17s, attacked shipping in the Andaman Islands on April 2, 1942. In June the retreating bombers were transferred to the Middle East. The first B-24 strike in China was from Chengtu on October 21, by the 436th Squadron of the 7th Bomb Group. A new B-24 group, the 308th, flew its first mission with Chennault's 14th Air Force on May 4, eighteen Liberators crossing the Gulf of Tonkin to attack tar-

This 28th Bomb Group Liberator returned from a mission to find its Aleutian base fog bound, landed elsewhere. (USAF)

"V-Victor" of 37 Squadron, RAF, moments before bombs cut off the 2 prop and knocked out the upper turret over Monfalcone, Italy in March 1945. The aircraft flew 300 miles back to base. (Imperial War Museum)

gets on Hainan. The 308th was different to other B-24 groups in a very special and highly undesirable way — to operate in China they had to acquire all their supplies by shuttling them over the treacherous Hump route.

Between October 1944 and May 1945 the 7th Bomb Group was involved in mining ports and disrupting enemy communications. The radio-controlled Azon bomb, introduced in December 1944, made this type of work considerably easier and considerably

This is what happened on Kwajalein when the left tyre of this 30th Bomb Group B-24 blew out on take-off, in August 1944. (USAF)

40

"Umbriago" of the 492nd Bomb Group, over Germany on July 16, 1944, carries a combination of early and late Second Air Division fin symbols. (USAF)

less expensive. It was very effective against railroad lines and bridges, but because of the specialist nature of the operations and the training and equipment involved, the 493rd Squadron of the 7th Group was the sole operator. The bombs were dropped singly, from eight to ten thousand feet, and the fact that one mission destroyed four bridges with four bombs is an adequate testimonial. On the first Azon attack on December 27, the Pyinmana Bridge carrying the railroad track linking Rangoon with Mandalay was destroyed, a feat which had eluded bombers and fighters for two years.

Eight planes over Bougainville on November 16, 1943 were the first effort of the first new B-24 group in the Pacific, the 90th, soon to be joined by the "Flying Circus," the 380th. In February of the following year the 307th arrived at Espiritu Santo, and later they and the "Bomber Barons," the 5th Bomb Group, moved to hard-won Guadalcanal to back up the Bougainville invasion. A few months earlier, in August, ten special snooper SB-24s had joined the 5th's 394th Squadron and on low-level operations up the Slot they sank more shipping at night than the rest of the B-24s could during the day.

A Liberator Mark VI of Coastal Command's 220 Squadron. The underwing Leigh Light of a sister Liberator appears at the top of the photo. (Imperial War Museum)

42   *"Betsy" of the 90th Bomb Group is heading for Wewak, New Guinea, in February 1944. (USAF)*

Aircraft of the 458th Bomb Group on the way out at Horsham St. Faith, Norfolk, on Christmas Eve, 1944. (USAF)

The Seventh Air Force flew its first mission since General Tinker's luckless June 6 four plane mission to Wake — and General Landon's more successful mission with the three remaining LB-30s two weeks

A Liberator of the Australian 24 Squadron going down in flames while attacking the Jap cruiser Isuzu near Sumba Island in 1945. (RAAF)

later — on December 22, 1942. Twenty-six 307th Bomb Group B-24Ds attacked Wake, led by Colonel William A. Matheny. They took the enemy by surprise, coming in over the target between 2500 and 8000 feet and the only damage they took was a couple of holes in Matheny's ship.

The 7th's B-24s moved to the Gilberts islands, still scarred by their bombs, in winter 1943, and supported the invasion of the Marshalls with 1000 lb and 2000 lb "atoll busters," capable of cracking open the type of installations that had withstood the aerial onslaught on the Gilberts.

Rabaul and Truk, two fabled and strong Japanese bases were neutralized and bypassed. The intensive assault on Rabaul began on October 12, 1943, when the 43rd and 90th Groups, accompanied by P-38s and B-25s, flew from Port Moresby. For four months the New Britain stronghold was pounded, but the pounding was not one-sided. Both of the 5th's groups and the 13th's 5th and 307th had their hands full at Rabaul.

Truk became target number one. The 7th's 30th Bomb Group made the initial land-based attack on

"Burma Bound" of the 451st Bomb Group, 15th Air Force, in trouble near Munich in December 1944. (USAF)

the night of March 14, flying from the Gilberts with a staging stop at Kwajalein. The first plans found the lights burning, workers working, and all got home. The 307th followed two weeks later with the first daylight attack.

The 11th Bomb Group moved to Kwajalein in April 1944 and joined the 30th. On April 18 five 30th Bomb Group B-24s teamed with Navy PB4Y-1s for a photo recon and bombing attack on the Marianas, adding to their "firsts." After the Marianas fell, the

"Redwing", a PB4Y-2 Privateer", became "Indian Made" with a small, flimsy, but strategically placed abdominal veil, later in her career. (Birdsall Collection)

This and the following three pictures are taken from a group of K20 negs taken by a 26th Bomb Squadron, 11th Bomb Group photographer. (Beresford B. Gilkes Collection)

Two B-24s, one from the 26th Squadron, the other from the 98th, drone through scattered cloud on their way to the target. (Gilkes Collection)

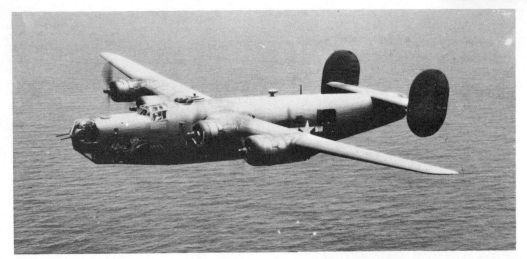

"K Lucy II", a nine mission veteran from the 26th Squadron, serial number 42-109865. (Gilkes Collection)

The target. (Gilkes Collection)

Eniwetok, April 18, 1944. An 11th Bomb Group B-24 cleans up her gear as ground crew prepare other ships for an attack on Truk. (USAF)

30th and 11th Groups moved there, but occasionally dropped in on Truk until the middle of 1945, dropping cautionary bombs on its shattered installations.

Borneo, and the Balikpapan oil refineries, was barely within the range of Australian based Liberators, but nine 380th Group aircraft struck there in August 1944 on a seventeen hour round flight. Of necessity, they struck lightly. When Noemfoor airstrip in New Guinea came into allied hands, the target was reduced to a fourteen hour, 2350 mile journey to be flown with 3590 gallons of fuel and 2,500 lbs of bombs. Experts from Consolidated and Pratt & Whitney pooled their talents with AAF officers to devise an intricate and precise flight plan. Working to an exact timetable, the utmost performance would be wrung from the bombers by shifting weight and removing it altogether. After four hours the auxiliary fuel in the bomb bay tanks would be

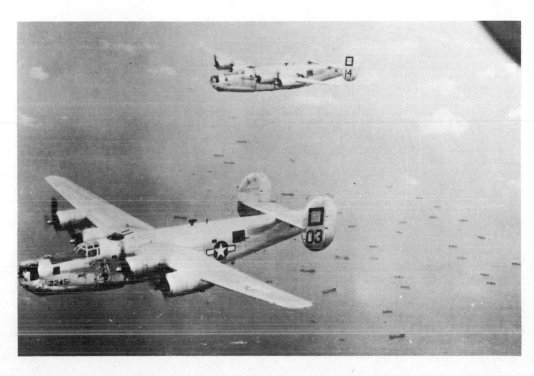

B-24s of the 5th Bomb Group's 23rd Squadron passing over the invasion fleet off the coast of Borneo on July 2, 1945. (USAF)

A B-24 of the 281st Squadron, 465th Bomb Group, flying out of Pantanella, crosses the Alps, bound for southern Germany. (USAF)

transferred, after six and a half hours one waist gunner would move to the tail, and after nine hours two men would be moved forward to the flight deck. Ninety minutes from the target all that remained of each ship's 1362 pounds of .50 caliber ammunition was to be jettisoned.

At 4:00 a.m. on September 30, 1944 seventy-two 5th and 13th Air Force B-24s from the 5th, 307th and 90th Groups began leaving Noemfoor. Seventy made the target, but four 307th planes were shot down, the crews of three and half the crew of the fourth being snatched from the Pacific by PBYs.

The most rewarding raid on Balikpapan was the fourth on October 14, with fighter escort. The price for neutralizing Balikpapan was twenty-two bombers — considerably less for what was often called "the Ploesti of the Pacific."

Fifty-seven B-24s attacked Davao on September 1, 1944, opening up their portion of the Philippines campaign. When Leyte was invaded the next month the B-24s lent a hand from Morotai and in November the new 494th Group was operating from Angaur in the Palaus, followed by the 22nd Bomb Group in December. While they hammered Manila's enemy airfields the 43rd, 90th, 380th and 307th Groups were hitting Formosa and hounding the enemy in every conceivable place and way.

The 11th and 30th Groups, on Guam and Saipan,

A Ford-built C-109 of the IX Troop Carrier Command in England in December 1944. Aerial tankers, they supplied the advancing ground forces in Europe. (USAF)

were after the Bonins, but the honor of being first over Iwo Jima was claimed by two VB-109 PB4Y-1s that landed on Saipan on July 12 and flew 650 miles to the north to attack Iwo the next day. Two VPB-116 aircraft from Tinian put on a rather spectacular display near Iwo Jima; enemy air strength there was acknowledged, and accordingly Navy planes patrolling the sector dropped down to the deck about seventy-five miles from the island in order to proceed, at around 100 feet, to within a couple of miles of the island before being discovered. Gaining a few hundred feet they would pass quickly over the island and take a look at what the Japanese were doing. The two VPB-116 aircraft were searching for

"Judith Ann" of the 459th Bomb Group arriving at Poltava shuttle base in Russia on April 12, 1945. (USAF)

"Lady Kaye" of the 494th Bomb Group's 867th Squadron, equipped with manual ventral guns in place of the ball turret, heads out on a mission to the Gulf of Davao in February 1945. The 494th was known as "Kelly's Cobras". They entered combat on November 3, 1944 and were the first AAF Liberators over Japan from Okinawa, taking off from there less than 24 hours after arriving from the Palaus. The target was Omura, and all forty-eight planes came back. (USAF)

another Liberator that had failed to return and they suddenly found themselves set upon by eight fighters. During the heated contest that developed six of the Japanese were shot down and the two survivors, no *Kamikazes*, headed back to Iwo.

The B-24s of the 11th and 30th paved the way for the Marines with round-the-clock bomb and napalm raids and by D-Day on February 19, 1945

they had dropped over 5,500 tons of bombs on the forbidding island.

The capture of the Ryukus in April put the B-24s within range of the Japanese home islands and in July the 11th moved up to Okinawa to join Privateers that had arrived there on April 22. The 494th followed from the Palaus, and squadrons of the 22nd, 90th and 380th, while the 43rd set up on Ie

"Kuuipo's" crew waits under her wing before a mission against the Palaus in November 1944. The plane belongs to the 494th Group's 864th Squadron. (USAF)

RAF Liberators abandoned in India. Those in the foreground are from 99 Squadron, which flew its last mission on August 12, 1945. (George Cull via Philip Moyes)

Shima. They began striking targets in the Shanghai and Hangchow areas of China and on Kyushu, preparing for what everyone knew must be the bloodiest phase of the war — the invasion of Japan.

To gain operational experience with the B-24, two special Royal Australian Air Force Flights were formed, flying with the 43rd Group at Nadzab and the 380th Group at Darwin. The pay-off came with the invasion of Borneo. Attacks on Borneo, Java and Celebes began twenty days before the first landing, at Tarakan on May 1. 21 and 24 Squadrons, brought from Darwin to Morotai, flew against Borneo with 13th and 5th Air Force squadrons and 23 and 25 Squadrons hit Java and other key points in the area. Six weeks later the second Australian landing was made, on Labuan Island on Borneo's west coast, and the third landing, at Balikpapan, was launched on July 1. Two RAAF composite squadrons, with B-24s from 21, 23 and 24 Squadrons followed Thirteenth Air Force Liberators across the beaches and were in turn followed by B-24s from the Fifth Air Force. Nothing on the tortured shore was left intact, and

Commander Norman Miller's VB-109 PB4Y-1 "Thunder Mug" sank or damaged 66 ships and shot down fifteen enemy aircraft before the Japanese shot out her brakes over Puluwat. (USN)

seventeen assault waves landed without a casualty. The RAAF Liberators' job was not quite over — they were conscripted as artillery spotters until tiny strips could be built for the more suitable Austers. Three B-24s were lost carrying out observation flights, one of them at 200 feet, before their impromptu duty was over.

Flying one of the final B-24 missions of World War II fifty-three aircraft made a devastating fire attack on Kurume, their incendiaries searing out 28% of the city. The date was August 11, 1945, four days after the atomic bombing of Hiroshima, which, followed by a similar attack on Nagasaki, ended the war with Japan.

It has been impossible in these few thousand words to chronicle the full story of Consolidated's Liberator at war. As a compromise, some of the highlights, some of the types of war and some of the allied units using B-24s have been assembled. With the photographs, they are intended to convey, at least in part, the immensity of the B-24s' contribution to the victory that ended its usefulness.

This 90th Bomb Group B-24D crashed at Moonlight Creek in the north of Australia in December 1942, and still lies there. (Mirror Newspapers)

— USAF

Above a blanket of cloud, the 44th Bomb Group B-24D "Princess", 42-63962, heads toward a European target . . .

ESCAPE INTO SWEDEN

During World War II sixty one USAAF Liberators found a place to rest their war weary bodies in neutral Sweden. The first there was a B-24D from the 93rd Bomb Group on October 9, 1943, the last the 446th Bomb Group's "Ladcn Maiden" on April 2 of 1945. Many of the details of these aircraft have yet to come to light, but let's look at just a few.

There was "War Baby" from the 93rd at Orebro on November 18, 1943. "Hello Natural" from the 448th, "Princess" from the 44th, "Jiggs" from the 446th, and "Mistah Chick" and "Princess Konocti" from the 389th. The 492nd Bomb Group was represented by eight aircraft, among them "Silver Witch", "Say When", "Sknappy" and "Boulder Buff".

Her crew did not know that on May 29, 1944 they would not be going back to Shipdam in England . . .

Instead, they went to Bulltofta, Sweden, port in a storm to thirty-one Liberators between March 1944 and January 1945.

— via Nick Nilsson

— via Nick Nilsson

Two views of 42-63971, a B-24D coded GJ-W from the 44th Bomb Group, which crashlanded at Trollhattan on November 18, 1943. (Swedish Air Staff Photos)

Above: "Hello Natural" of the 448th Bomb Group force-landed in Sweden on March 6, 1944. Fifty-nine Liberators made Sweden between October 1943 and April 1945 — the biggest day was June 20, 1944, when sixteen came in. (Nick Nilsson)

Right: "Princess Konocti" landed at Halmstad on June 20, 1944. The aircraft, 42-100190 of the 389th Bomb Group, was returned to England in June 1945. (via Nick Nilsson)

Below: 42-40610 from the 93rd Bomb Group in bad shape at Rinkaby, October 9, 1943. (Swedish Air Staff Photo)

Bottom: An early model B-24H, stripped of armament, at Orebro. This 392nd Bomb Group aircraft landed there on November 18, 1943. (Swedish Air Staff Photo)

THE LUCKLESS "LADY BE GOOD"

Tragedy in war is no rarity. War could almost be called a succession of tragedies combining to become the ultimate tragedy.

When Lt. William J. Hatton lifted the 376th Bomb Group's *Lady Be Good* from the strip at Soluch, Libya he could not have known that he was heading into a sixteen year mystery.

An oil prospecting team in a C-47 first saw the

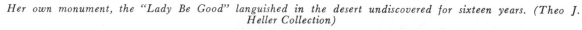

Her own monument, the "Lady Be Good" languished in the desert undiscovered for sixteen years. (Theo J. Heller Collection)

twisted wreck 350 miles south of Benghazi in November 1958. The pilot reported the sighting, but it aroused little interest. He also recorded the site on maps that would be used by a ground team exploring the area.

A year later they came upon the aircraft with its borrowed Gershwin name. The aircraft was empty, but only of the crew. There was water, and even a flask of coffee. They found the navigator's log, and this answered many questions. The ship had been on a mission to Naples Harbor on April 4, 1943.

This was enough to begin the laborious task of tracing the aircraft. The crew had arrived in North Africa in March. On April 4 twenty-five B-24s left Soluch in two sections. By the time they were thirty miles south of the target it was dark, and the second section, reduced to four planes, decided to turn back.

One B-24 ran out of fuel and landed on Malta, two made it to Soluch, and the *Lady Be Good* . . .

A little after midnight Hatton broke radio silence and called Benghazi. He asked for an inbound bearing, and got it. He was on a direct line from Naples to Benghazi. But they had crossed the coast without knowing it, and they were flying away from Benghazi, into the Libyan Sand Sea.

The fuel finally ran out, and Hatton ordered his crew to jump, and followed them. The *Lady Be Good* drifted down.

In 1959, extensive searching by ground and with helicopters revealed marker triangles indicating that

The bodies of five of the crewmen (Theo. J. Heller Collection)

the crew had made their way north. Twenty-five miles from the Sand Sea the tracks ended. Four months after it began, the search was abandoned.

Then in February 1960 oil prospectors found the most important link in the chain. This was co-pilot Robert Toner's diary. It told how eight of the crew had managed to join up with each other, unaware of their impending fate. In the morning of Monday, April 5 they began their trek, with one flask of water, a little food, and their parachute canopies.

When night came the oven became a refrigerator. They found they could not sleep. So they decided to

walk, and kept going until 11:30 the following morning. By Wednesday morning they knew they could not keep going much longer. Half their water, taken at the rate of a capfull per day per man, had gone. They kept praying.

The following day they saw the Libyan Sand Sea — they had come over seventy miles. They sank into the soft sand, and clouds of it blew into their eyes, blinding them.

On Friday only three had the strength to carry on — Guy Shelley, Rip Ripslinger, the engineer, and Vernon Moore. They would try to find help, while the

other five waited. The next morning they prayed again, forlornly searching the sky for a search plane, knowing in their hearts that death would be their deliverance. Toner's diary told of their terrible pain, and ended with his final entry, on Monday, April 11: "No help yet, very cold nite."

The five bodies were found on an upward slope in the dunes. The oil prospectors began searching for the rest of the crew. But they found nothing.

Then months later, prospectors again found another link. Two more bodies. As one had fallen, the other had gone on, carrying the last of their hopes into an unrelenting desert. Ripslinger had got twenty miles, Shelley seven miles further, and Moore's body was never found. It is unlikely that he would have lasted as long as his two comrades.

Of all the B-24 groups of World War II, the 376th, the "Liberandos," has left the most for posterity. In addition to their display aircraft, the 512th Squadron's *Strawberry Bitch*, the United States Air Force Museum in Ohio has on display the *Lady Be Good's* canteen, compass, maps and charts, the navigator's log, one of the props, and a fifty caliber machine gun.

THE SAGA OF THE "STRAWBERRY BITCH"

In all the United States there is but one B-24D. This aircraft, 42-72843, is permanently parked among several of her contemporaries at the United States Air Force Museum at Wright-Patterson Air Force Base.

Before arriving at the Museum in 1959, the *Strawberry Bitch* had spent thirteen years in storage at Davis-Monthan AFB's boneyard in the Arizona desert.

Her skin still carries the scars of fifty-nine missions with the 512th Bomb Squadron of the 376th Bomb Group. Let's go back to one of those missions now, with Lt. George Webster, navigator of the ship on a mission to Eleusis Aerodrome, near Athens, Greece. The date: October 5, 1943.

The "Strawberry Bitch" with the
376th's 515th Squadron in Italy.
(Air Force Museum)

"We were in the number three ship in the third element of 'B' section. On the outgoing trip there was nothing to arouse any emotion other than the usual tension before the firing began.

"We sighted land and I alerted the crew over the interphone and kept the boys on the lookout. After reaching our IP we approached the target on a heading of 93° and our first indication of any enemy resistance was the small, wicked looking black puffs of smoke that appeared ahead of us and seemed to be directly in our path. Those small deadly balls somehow relieved the nervous tension and we settled down for the actual bombing run.

"Up in the nose, bombardier William Jones and I were busy getting set up for the signal from our element leader to drop our bombs on the already smoking target. The first wave of aircraft passed over the target and then we could see the bomb bay doors of our leader's plane slowly open.

"During the few seconds taken to drop our bombs we weren't aware of the constant lurching of the ship as flak exploded close to our plane — too close for comfort. At last the cry of 'bombs away' came over the interphone and broke the spell. At once every member of the crew reported bomb bursts seen, and fighter activity. The formation, after leaving the target area, swung in a slow turn to the left and headed for home.

"Once the homeward journey began, both 'A' and 'B' sections of the formation swung together for mutual protection. No sooner had we regained our position than we heard the cry 'fighters at 6 o'clock' from our tail gunner. That put us all on edge immediately.

"The first indication of fighters came when a Messerschmidt 109, going at tremendous speed, came

Taking the aircraft out of storage involved considerably more effort than putting her in. (Air Force Museum)

down past the nose, hardly at wing tip length from us. After that the interphone crackled and another cry of fighters at three and six o'clock. I heard the rattling of machine guns on our ship and saw the flame bursting from the gun muzzles of the planes on all sides of us. The fighters made two passes at us and then decided to hang on to our element.

"Our interphones were strangely silent and Dan Rice was doing a swell job of keeping us in formation. What happened next I found out later from the rest of the crew. Evidently the attacking planes held off for a few moments and lined up behind us in rows of six. At the signal from their leader they bored in on us. The lead ship of our element suddenly seemed to stop and stand still as though a giant hand had pressed against the nose. Rice throttled back to hold

formation, but couldn't hold back too much for fear of stalling out. We looked around for the ship flying the leader's other wing but he too had fallen back, apparently hit. The two aircraft, numbers 72 and 64, were rapidly losing ground. Eight parachutes spilled out the bomb bay doors of 64 but 72's pilot was fighting a losing battle trying to keep the plane under control. He couldn't, and the plane slowly went into a tight spin to the right. I saw one parachute and watched the left rudder come off. In moments it had plunged out of sight. I went back to my gunnery and heard another attack on our tail called in. Sergeant Collier in the tail knocked one down, and then we heard, or rather felt, the impact of the shells hitting our stabilizer and another hitting the number one prop. The exploding shells were flying

Stripped back to bare metal the aircraft loses a lot of character. (Air Force Museum)

Freshly repainted in essentially the same markings she carried twenty-three years ago, the only B-24D in the world is all set to claim a well-deserved place at the museum. (Air Force Museum)

all around us and our top turret man, Sergeant Ralph Haberman, was knocked unconscious by concussion and shell fragments. The last shell exploded so close to the nose that it put a number of holes in the turret and side of the fuselage. Dan Rice decided the fighter had our number and he was going to make sure the day's tally wouldn't include us. He poured the gas on and we crept in under the wing of the leading section like a crippled duck.

"In the meantime Haberman had climbed dazedly out of the hit turret and our radio man took over. Rice came to look Haberman over and make him as comfortable as possible.

"After the fighters had finished with us they picked on the last element and shot their leader down in flames. The rest of the element came up fast and joined in the massed formation, and the Nazi planes veered off and headed for home too. After a quick check that everything was still in flying shape Rice relaxed a little.

"The rest of the trip was uneventful and we made Berca by dark. After landing we checked up on the extent of the damage and suddenly realized just how lucky we were to be back safe and sound; the two holes in the right wing were large enough to bail gasoline out of, one hole in the left wing travelled from the trailing edge and came out the leading edge, you could put a football through the hole in the left stabilizer, all of our antennae were shot away, the top turret was holed, and the number one propeller had a hole in it that we were scared to look at. Still, I guess all's well that ends well . . ."

That was the *Strawberry Bitch's* fifth mission.

The aircraft flew fifty-four more; first from Soluch, Libya, then in November 1943 from San Pancrazio in Italy. Her nine months of combat operations were spent attacking targets in Italy, Greece, Austria, France, Germany, Hungary, Bulgaria and Rumania. In 1946 *Strawberry Bitch* was put into storage at Davis-Monthan, and rested undisturbed for thirteen years, until 1959, when her faded paintwork was scraped off, renewed, and she was flown by Colonel Albert Shower to Wright-Patterson Air Forse Base via Bunker Hill AFB Indiana, arriving at the Air Force Museum on May 18, 1959. The aircraft is a B-24D-160-CO.

— All 6th PRG photos from the collections of the author and Merle Olmsted. 63

About the Author . . .

Steve Birdsall's historical interests range from the Conquistadores to old railroad locomotives, but his specialty is the airmen and aircraft of World War II. He has devoted years to accumulating aircraft photographs and data and to correspondence with wartime pilots. A member of such groups as the American Aviation Historical Society and the Air Force Historical Foundation, he is a prolific writer and has contributed numerous articles to historical journals and magazines around the world. His commentary on the B-24 is a natural follow-up to his "B-17 Flying Fortress," published in 1965.